Twelve Poems about Birds

Candlestick Press

Published by:
Candlestick Press,
DiVersity House, 72 Nottingham Road,
Arnold, Nottingham NG5 6LF
www.candlestickpress.co.uk

Design, typesetting, print and production by Diversity Creative
Marketing Solutions Ltd., www.diversitymarketing.co.uk

Illustrations © Jill Perry, 2010
Introduction © Jenny Swann, 2010

© Candlestick Press, 2010

First Published 2010
Reprinted 2011, 2013, 2015

ISBN 978 0 955 8944 9 7

Acknowledgements:
The publisher acknowledges with thanks Lynne Wycherley and
Shoestring Press for permission to print 'Bewick Swans arrive at
Ouse Washes', Collins Publishers and the author for 'The Quails' by
Francis Brett Young (copyright © Francis Brett Young) from *Poems
1916 - 1918* and Karin Koller for permission to print 'bird feeder'.
'Sandpiper' by Elizabeth Bishop (Copyright © Elizabeth Bishop) is
reprinted by permission of A M Heath and Co Ltd, Authors' Agents.

Where poets are no longer living, their dates are given.

Twelve Poems about Birds is dedicated to Roderick Thorne,
Ranger on Sanday (www.sandayorkney.co.uk), who taught me
all I know about birds, JS

Introduction

Down the centuries, countless poets have hitched a lift
on the wings of birds. Some of the earliest surviving
Anglo-Saxon poems describe the haunting calls of birds
as they accompany seafarers through the harsh realities of
their lives.

Twelve Poems about Birds (a baker's dozen, incidentally)
can only offer a glimpse of our rich heritage of bird poetry.
Some seminal poems have had to be left out – John Keats'
'Ode to a Nightingale' and Wallace Stevens' masterpiece,
'Thirteen Ways of Looking at a Blackbird' deserve
pamphlets of their own, for a start.

We hope that this small selection of poems will inspire you
to read on elsewhere – perhaps on rainy days when your
binoculars and field guides lie idle.

Some of the chosen poems will be familiar to readers and
some unfamiliar – either because they have fallen out of
fashion or because they are published here for the first time.

We kick off with a traditional rhyme, known in various
versions:

Magpies

One for sorrow,
Two for joy,
Three for a letter,
Four for a boy,
Five for a secret never to be told,
Six for silver,
Seven for gold.

Jenny Swann

Bewick Swans arrive at Ouse Washes

Just when I think the winter has won,
a black book closing

on pages of light,
and the darkness sways on its haunches

like an impatient bear
scooping up silver minnows,

I sense an agitation in the sky,
long Vs trailing like pennons.

Altocirrus, swans white
as the tundra they come from.

Their cries multiply. Their bodies
crash-land on the water

star after star after star.

Lynne Wycherley

Birds' Nests

The summer nests uncovered by autumn wind,
Some torn, others dislodged, all dark,
Everyone sees them: low or high in tree,
Or hedge, or single bush, they hang like a mark.

Since there's no need of eyes to see them with
I cannot help a little shame
That I missed most, even at eye's level, till
The leaves blew off and made the seeing no game.

'Tis a light pang. I like to see the nests
Still in their places, now first known,
At home and by far roads. Boys knew them not,
Whatever jays and squirrels may have done.

And most I like the winter nests deep-hid
That leaves and berries fell into:
Once a dormouse dined there on hazel-nuts,
And grass and goose-grass seeds found soil and grew.

Edward Thomas (1878 – 1917)

Sandpiper

The roaring alongside he takes for granted,
and that every so often the world is bound to shake.
He runs, he runs to the south, finical, awkward,
in a state of controlled panic, a student of Blake.

The beach hisses like fat. On his left, a sheet
of interrupting water comes and goes
and glazes over his dark and brittle feet.
He runs, he runs straight through it, watching his toes.

– Watching, rather, the spaces of sand between them,
where (no detail too small) the Atlantic drains
rapidly backwards and downwards. As he runs,
he stares at the dragging grains.

The world is a mist. And then the world is
minute and vast and clear. The tide
is higher or lower. He couldn't tell you which.
His beak is focussed; he is preoccupied,

looking for something, something, something.
Poor bird, he is obsessed!
The millions of grains are black, white, tan, and gray,
mixed with quartz grains, rose and amethyst.

Elizabeth Bishop (1911 – 1979)

The Darkling Thrush

I leant upon a coppice gate
   When Frost was spectre-gray,
And Winter's dregs made desolate
   The weakening eye of day.
The tangled bine-stems scored the sky
   Like strings of broken lyres,
And all mankind that haunted nigh
   Had sought their household fires.

The land's sharp features seemed to be
   The Century's corpse outleant,
His crypt the cloudy canopy,
   The wind his death-lament.
The ancient pulse of germ and birth
   Was shrunken hard and dry,
And every spirit upon earth
   Seemed fervourless as I.

At once a voice arose among
   The bleak twigs overhead
In a full-hearted evensong
   Of joy illimited,
An aged thrush, frail, gaunt, and small,
   In blast-beruffled plume,
Had chosen thus to fling his soul
   Upon the growing gloom.

So little cause for carolings
   Of such ecstatic sound
Was written on terrestrial things
   Afar or nigh around,
That I could think there trembled through
   His happy good-night air
Some blessed Hope, whereof he knew
   And I was unaware.

Thomas Hardy (1840 – 1928)

*The Windhover
To Christ our Lord

I caught this morning morning's minion, king –
  dom of daylight's dauphin, dapple-dawn-drawn Falcon, in his
    riding
Of the rolling level underneath him steady air, and striding
High there, how he rung upon the rein of a wimpling wing
In his ecstacy! then off, off forth on swing,
  As a skate's heel sweeps smooth on a bow-bend: the hurl and
    gliding
 . Rebuffed the big wind. My heart in hiding
Stirred for a bird, – the achieve of, the mastery of the thing!

Brute beauty and valour and act, oh, air, pride, plume, here
  Buckle! And the fire that breaks from thee then, a billion
Times told lovelier, more dangerous, O my chevalier!

No wonder of it: shéer plód makes plough down sillion
Shine, and blue-bleak embers, ah my dear,
  Fall, gall themselves, and gash gold-vermilion.

Gerard Manley Hopkins (1844 – 1889)

*Kestrel

The Wren

Why is the cuckoos melody prefered
And nightingales rich song so fondly praised
In poets ryhmes Is there no other bird
Of natures minstrelsy that oft hath raised
Ones heart to extacy and mirth as well
I judge not how anothers taste is caught
With mines theres other birds that bear the bell
Whose song hath crowds of happy memories brought
Such the wood Robin singing in the dell
And little Wren that many a time hath sought
Shelter from showers in huts where I did dwell
In early spring the tennant of the plain
Tenting my sheep and still they come to tell
The happy stories of the past again

The Happy Bird

The happy white throat on the sweeing bough
Swayed by the impulse of the gadding wind
That ushers in the showers of april – now
Singeth right joyously and now reclined
Croucheth and clingeth to her moving seat
To keep her hold – and till the wind for rest
Pauses – she mutters inward melodys
That seem her hearts rich thinkings to repeat
And when the branch is still – her little breast
Swells out in raptures gushing symphonys
And then against her blown wing softly prest
The wind comes playing an enraptured guest
This way and that she swees – till gusts arise
More boisterous in their play – when off she flies

John Clare (1793 – 1864)

Note: These versions follow the spelling and grammar given
in *John Clare, Major Works*, OUP, 1984.

bird feeder

an everyday sighting: so usual: so unremarkable: so unsurprising

yet

whenever one flies to the feeder which h
                                        a
                                        n
                                        g
                                        s

                                    out   side
                                    m   y
                                    win   dow
           p
i look u   observe its busy peckings, its over-the-wing-glances

feel joy to be so visited   and   it doesn't matter

        robin   blue   coal
if it's a   a   tit   a   tit   if
           or   or   or

                                at *
2/or/3/or/more   happen/to/come   all* the
                                 same*
                               * time
                                 *

                  the emotion is just the same

Karin Koller

The Quails

(In the south of Italy the peasants put out the eyes of a captured quail so that its cries may attract the flocks of spring migrants into their nets, FBY)

All through the night
I have heard the stuttering call of a blind quail,
A caged decoy, under a cairn of stones,
Crying for light as the quails cry for love.

Other wanderers,
Northward from Africa winging on numb pinions,
        dazed
With beating winds and the sobbing of the sea,
Hear, in a breath of sweet land-herbage, the call
Of the blind one, their sister. . . .
Hearing, their fluttered hearts
Take courage, and they wheel in their dark flight,
Knowing that their toil is over, dreaming to see
The white stubbles of Abruzzi smitten with dawn,
And spilt grain lying in the furrows, the squandered
        gold
That is the delight of quails in their spring mating.

Land-scents grow keener,
Penetrating the dank and bitter odour of brine
That whitens their feathers;
Far below, the voice of their sister calls them
To plenty, and sweet water, and fulfilment.
Over the pallid margin of dim seas breaking,
Over the thickening in the darkness that is land,
They fly. Their flight is ended. Wings beat no more.
Downward they drift, one by one, like dark petals,
Slowly, listlessly falling
Into the mouth of horror:
The nets. . .

Where men come trampling and crying with bright
    lanterns,
Plucking their weak, entangled claws from the meshes
    of net,
Clutching the soft brown bodies mottled with olive,
Crushing the warm, fluttering flesh, in hands stained
    with blood,
Till their quivering hearts are stilled, and the bright
    eyes,
That are like a polished agate, glaze in death.

But the blind one, in her wicker cage, without ceasing
Haunts this night of spring with her stuttering call,
Knowing nothing of the terror that walks in darkness,
Knowing only that some cruelty has stolen the light
That is life, and that she must cry until she dies.

I, in the darkness,
Heard, and my heart grew sick. But I know that
    to-morrow
A smiling peasant will come with a basket of quails
Wrapped in vine-leaves, prodding them with blood-
    stained fingers,
Saying, 'Signore, you must cook them thus, and thus,
With a sprig of basil inside them.' And I shall thank
    him,
Carrying the piteous carcases into the kitchen
Without a pang, without shame.

'Why should I be ashamed? Why should I rail
Against the cruelty of men? Why should I pity,
Seeing that there is no cruelty which men can imagine
To match the subtle dooms that are wrought against
    them
By blind spores of pestilence: seeing that each of us,
Lured by dim hopes, flutters in the toils of death
On a cold star that is spinning blindly through space
Into the nets of time?'

So cried I, bitterly thrusting pity aside,
Closing my lids to sleep. But sleep came not,
And pity, with sad eyes,
Crept to my side, and told me
That the life of all creatures is brave and pityful
Whether they be men, with dark thoughts to vex them,
Or birds, wheeling in the swift joys of flight,
Or brittle ephemerids, spinning to death in the haze
Of gold that quivers on dim evening waters;
Nor would she be denied.
The harshness died
Within me, and my heart
Was caught and fluttered like the palpitant heart
Of a brown quail, flying
To the call of her blind sister,
And death, in the spring night.

Francis Brett Young (1884 – 1954)

"Hope' is the thing with feathers'

'Hope' is the thing with feathers –
That perches in the soul –
And sings the tune without the words –
And never stops – at all –

And sweetest – in the Gale – is heard –
And sore must be the storm –
That could abash the little Bird
That kept so many warm –

I've heard it in the chillest land –
And on the strangest Sea –
Yet, never, in Extremity,
It asked a crumb – of Me.

Emily Dickinson (1830 – 1886)

The Ptarmigan

The Ptarmigan is strange,
As strange as he can be;
Never sits on ptelephone poles
Or roosts upon a ptree.
And the way he ptakes pto spelling
Is the strangest thing pto me.

Anon

Limericks

There was an Old Man, on whose nose
Most birds of the air could repose;
But they all flew away, at the closing of day,
Which relieved that Old Man and his nose.

There was an Old Man with a beard,
Who said, "It is just as I feared! –
Two Owls and a Hen, four Larks and a Wren,
Have all built their nests in my beard."

Edward Lear (1812 – 1888)